Alpenglow Miracles:
Fire Dance of Wonder

Photos and Poems
by
Dwayne Cole

Alpenglow Miracles: Fire Dance of Wonder

ISBN: Softcover 978-1-955581-29-5

Copyright © 2021 by Dwayne Cole

All rights reserved. No part of this book may be reproduced or transmitted in any form or by any means, electronic or mechanical, including photocopying, recording, or by any information storage and retrieval system, without permission in writing from the publisher.

Parson's Porch Books is an imprint of Parson's Porch *&* Company (PP*&*C) in Cleveland, Tennessee. PP*&*C is an innovative organization which raises money by publishing books of noted authors, representing all genres. Its face and voice is **David Russell Tullock** (dtullock@parsonsporch.com).

Parson's Porch *&* Company *turns books into bread & milk* by sharing its profits with the poor.

www.parsonsporch.com

Alpenglow Miracles

Dedication

This book is dedicated to all lovers of nature.
When we walk into an Alpenglow sunrise, we walk as one—
Inspired by the miracle of being created afresh every morning.

When we ski into winter,
stand in glow of Aurora,
be still and listen,
hear Muse whispering secrets,

We are one with nature
and are all part of Alpenglow Miracles:
Fire Dance of Wonder
Sunrise of hope!

Preface: Grounded in Mystery

If you shape God in your own image, you will not understand my animated participation with our earthly surroundings and the use of ancient mythology and art to fully experience the beauty of life. Please do not read this as a criticism, but as a plea for oneness grounded in mystery that does not rest in the triumph of any one culture or creed.

The human craving for connection with that which is within our psyche, yet beyond us, has never been greater. We will not find peace that passes all understanding until we rest as one with the unifying Mind or Spirit that is at home deep within this mysterious and wild universe and at the same time in our own psyche, luring us to higher values.

The old puritanical spirit that disdains all earthly existence as sinful and has led to a careless depletion of our natural resources needs to be replaced with faithful stewardship that says, eternity is not elsewhere, not just out or up there some day, eternity is here now in adventurous hope.

> So I will do my part to save this beautiful world,
> to be attuned to creative advance,
> the hope and lure for enrichment,
> for our present and future generations,
> for we are all one.

Introduction

*The light in Alaska in particular is so beautiful.
So beautiful! Such incredible light."* Sebastiao Salgado

Far in Alaska,
foothills of the Chugach range,
grandparents caring for their family
found solace and tender love.

Alpenglow-ology was born—
sunrises and sunsets said,
"Photograph me,
write a poem about me."

Immense loveliness
shining through nature
brings mornings full of joy
and evenings so glorious-wild.

The mountains and skies,
the sun, moon, and stars,
the alpenglow clouds,
each a miracle of love.

Wisdom comes
in the sun magic world
in taking the gifts that are given—
Beauty, truth, goodness, and kindness.

The light in Alaska is so beautiful,
so very beautiful!

As the sun rises licking the ice crystals,
turning them purple, mauve, and golden,
I begin to muse—

What is time?
Can you crawl into it?

Jacob's dream ladder
would be nice!

In these awe inspiring moments—
Time does stand still.

The world becomes so beautiful
our soul cracks open.

Letting the glory in!

Aurora Haiku

Awake to art show
Drapes to purple room drawn
Sunrise glamour dance

At sunrise the sky
Is painted in golden colors
And joyfully dances

Alpenglow Miracles

Alpenglow starts like this:
as the sun awakes, pulling back the black drapes,
sprays of light splash up around the mountain peaks.

Golden tongue licking ice crystals
leaves drippings painting the sky with
pink, rosy, and purple delight.

Standing on tiptoes, my heart leaps with joy
at the aura, of light in the sun magic world.
Be still, my soul.
Have faith.
Goodness is everywhere!

Part II

As the sun rises licking the ice crystals,
turning them purple, mauve, and golden,
I begin to muse—

What is time?
Can you crawl into it?

Jacob's dream ladder
would be nice!

In these awe inspiring moments—
Time does stand still.

The world becomes so beautiful
our soul cracks open.

Letting the glory in!

Northern Lights

Morning comes for all living things,
as does the night.

Only the lucky few
see the dazzling display of Auroral lights.

To see this Northern wonder
in the night time sky

is like finding your lover
standing at the door

singing a romantic tune.
Please come in.

My heart has been yearning
for your magic colors.

Oh, please come in.
Shine in my life again and again.

Grounded in Mystery

Hestia, Greek goddess of the hearth,
sweeps the mountains with gold dust.
The clouds blush purple.
with envy and desire.

She waves her broom
like a wand,
and fire blazes in
the evening clouds.

Come, Hestia,
Let your emerald necklace
turn into sparkling stars
to light our eyes.

Sunlight Is Precious Gold

The lure of gold

drew many prospectors

to seek fortune in Alaska.

Some died in the pursuit.

A few found their dreams fulfilled.

The lucky ones

established homesteads

and found true enrichment

in Alaska's golden scenes.

Seeking a Haven

I've seen this before, in fact, many times,
but it is never ho hum. An always fresh scene
from the artist's palette, a sneak view of one peak
in the 250 mile Chugach range.
I snapped the picture by my condo.
When I viewed the scene I saw that I had captured
the raven of Alaskan myth,

      tilting, leaning,
    into the updraft of warm air,
      etching a black y
    in the golden-eye sunset sky.
    Speed an obvious joy,
the vibration of air around its flattened pennaceous
    and plumulaceous feathers
 whispers a faithful prayer of gratitude.
     Seeing. Sensing.
    My soul, seeking a haven
    from the world's craven,
pusillanimous ways, joins in the prayer.
  If this is not prayer from a raven,
      a wise maven,
    I don't know what is!

(In my poetry, I try not to use big words that might cause the reader to stop and wonder the meaning, maybe look up in a dictionary or ask Siri for more fun. Since this poem is about the wise raven, maven, I thought it appropriate to use a few new words and see the raven wink approval).

Hitch a Ride

Swing low,

spinning lenticular clouds,

stacking like pancakes above a plate of glass

with mountains of cream.

As mystifying as

Ezekiel's chariot of fire,

let me hitch a ride,

spinning, spinning,

higher, higher,

riding joy,

like a child

dancing heavenward!

Return like the prophet,

seeing, loving,

with twinkling eyes, gentle hands

and a new purpose.

Wings of Fire

Swing lower sweet alpenglow

shining like Ezekiel's chariot—

I yearn to be lifted into your wings of fire!

Let your lasso of light

Curl about my head

Let me spin higher, higher, higher

like a seraphim

into heaven's azure skies,

hear sun rise love songs of angels

return with twinkling eyes, gentle hands,

tender heart!

Portal of Heaven

The mountains draw me

to the highest peaks

to see where the world ends and heaven begins.

I understand why the poets of olden days

climbed the highest peaks,

opened every celestial door.

Unless we believe

the portal of heaven is near,

how will we find where the world ends

and heaven begins?

What if death is not closing our eyes in darkness

but stepping into

a golden sunrise!

Lifted by the translucent light

of new eyes seeing a new day

carried by the transforming cloud

into heaven's glorious way.

In the Clouds

My books,

photos, and poems are in the iCloud.

All of my life seems to be

moving toward the clouds.

Hope entwined in the web with ignorance,

fear with wisdom.

When my biography is written,

let me be lifted to lenticular clouds.

Enclosed in goodness

where I can smile down tenderly—

On my family and loved ones!

But please wait a little longer,

my story is not finished.

I want to show more kindness

on this side of the clouds.

Here grandchildren are watching me

compose poems of loving kindness.

Bronze Britches

Evening sun on the Chugach

dresses the birch trees in bronze britches

giving each tree tongues of fire

to sing songs of praise!

I join in the chorus fanning the flame

of adoration and thanksgiving.

Photo by my friend, G.W. Reid

Love is Fleeting

Moon kisses the dark blue lips of the night-time sky

bringing some color back

The affair will be brief

love waits on no one

Gather your rose buds while you may

Old Time is a flying

The flower that smiles today

Tomorrow will be fading

Use your time wisely

Gather the wedding flowers

Marry while you may

Sun will soon be rising

Let your love bloom

Lest it be a faint memory

Heaven's Glory

I go into nature

for solace and find healing,

broken and find wholeness.

I go out pulled in many directions and

return home peaceably centered

in God's grace and love.

Thank you, God,

for the many gifts of nature.

Your window revealing heaven's glory.

A Star Shining Bright

Standing on the cusp of Chugach

like a telescope with two legs,

I forget for a moment where I am.

For I have been transported

into the starry realm.

I am no longer

in this grounded place—

No longer confined

to the physical body.

I have become a heavenly body.

A star shining bright!

Finally coming back

to the snow covered mountain

I go home with star dust

in my soul shining bright.

Star Fire

Through eons of evolutionary time

Mother Nature has carved sparkling jewels

from uncut diamonds.

All of nature at times glows

like star fire inside frozen rime—

A Star Shining Bright.

Rise and shine!

Fog Crystals

Snow is falling,

turning the whole earth

into a winter wonderland.

Fog crystals form on the birches.

Snow turns spruces

into sparkling Christmas trees.

Redpolls don't mind.

They fluff their feathers into warm sleeping bags

and sleep through -20 degree nights.

With renewed hope,

I fluff my down bed covers for the night

and sleep tight.

Dance of Joy

I have been smitten

by Alpenglow wonder

Amazing wonder of the soul

Star dance of wonder

Star dance of joy

Night Colors

In Alaska we have entered winter solstice,
the darkest time of the year.
In the far North the sun will not rise again
for almost three months.
In Anchorage we do have
about five hours of light each day,
but a lot of snowy days
when you don't see the sun.
Yet, with the Alpenglow
sun rises and sunsets displaying
all the artist's palette of colors
and the rainbow ribbons
of the phenomenal northern lights,
I do think the night is often
more alive and colorful than the day.
Night time dreams are filled with color.
Paper birch trees are kaleidoscopic,
each twig a needle of shimmering polygons of light.
Seeing the Aurora all darkness falls away
revealing the mystery of creation.
Imagination builds for us
a world brimming with light.
The night dances with color
as heaven shines.

DayBreak Solace

Come sunrise
warm my face
with your caressing rays.
See me start my day in kindness
to keep some souls from aching
and some hearts from breaking.

Mountain Haibun

The mountains of Alaska create clouds called lenticular.

They can stack like pancakes,

and they can look like flying saucers at times.

Mother Nature can make them look like sunny side up fried eggs.

Thor, God of Thunder,

flipping pancakes on mountains

of whipped cream

Dawn Smiles

The alpenglow dawn smiles on snow capped mountains.

Wind gently blows through the trees and songs are whispered.

From spring's flower cup the magic brew sup.

On the wings of clouds and sun, a youthful zest is won.

A healing energy shines from all of nature's gifts.

Filling my soul with strength, courage, and hope.

My spirit raised,

I join the chorus of praise.

Clouds smiling warmly
Welcoming the new daybreak
Shine, shine, shine on me
Watch me respond with kindness
Smile warmly on all I meet

Glow-ology

As I sit mindfully
starting to write a poem,
I search for simple warm words.
Words to inspire.

My mind has a mind of its own.
It shouts philosophy, theology, psychology.
All the ologies of my past,
cry out to me.

Then, the sun starts to rise
The dance begins slowly and spreads,
A fire dance of wonder.
A star dance of joy.

A golden road is laid down on the water
I am transported by beauty.
Elfish star dust swirling around.
Glow-ology words abound.

Fire dance of wonder—
Lighting poetry's fire!

Aurora Lights

Morning comes for all living things, as does the night.

Only the lucky few

see the dazzling display

of Aurora lights.

To see this Northern wonder in the night time sky

is like finding your lover standing at the door

singing a romantic tune.

Please come in.

My heart has been yearning

for your magic colors.

Oh, please come in.

Shine in my life again and again.

Inside Auroras

countless galaxies spin

spin heaven and earth as one.

God of Love and Mercy

"I will be with you always"—Matthew 28:20

Since I have never seen You
I see You in every sunrise

Since I have never heard You
I hear You in every bird song

Since I have never held You
I hold You fast

Faith is Being
with You always

72

"The quieter you become
the more you are able to hear"—Rumi

Winter Tanka

Ski into winter
Stand in glow of Aurora
Be still and listen to moose
Crunching candy canes
Breathe the breath of perfection

Hear Muse whispering secrets

Great One Rules in Alaska

Denali sits beyond tundra
Ruling upon her throne
Great One is everywhere

Inviting all to come
Gaze upon beauty
Play around jeweled breast

Like prophets of old
Climb to highest peak
Hear Divine speak

See world with new eyes
Where earth ends
Heaven begins

In mountains
One always receives
More than one seeks

Cherubim sing alleluia
Alleluia to Great One
Who sees and feels everything

Tenderly saving all
That can be saved

Perishing, yet living for ever!

Part II

Denali sits beyond the tundra
Ruling upon her throne
The Great One is everywhere

Climb to the highest peak
Sit quietly
See the world with new eyes

Moses, poet of old, cradled as a baby
In a floating basket of bull rushes
Climbed Mount Sinai to hear the divine speak

To see where earth ends
and heaven begins
Cherubim sing alleluia

In going into the mountains
we always receive more than we give

I could get lost
And found in the Great One

Like the sages of old
I climb mountains to find God
The Poet of the world

Life is nurtured
Made new by Alpenglow miracles
Nature is the Poem.

(Photos show tundra with caribou, foothills with brown bear, and Denali—formerly know as Mt. McKinley. Denali is the highest mountain in North America with a summit elevation of 20,310 feet above sea level.

Size: 6,075,107 acres. Denali is 133 miles from Anchorage, and has about 600,000 visitors each year.)

I walk across the tundra toward Denali
My soul crying out to heaven's angels
Even the caribou grazing knows my sorrow
The brown bear having blueberry desert
Feels the pain trickling down my cheeks
There remains Denali, the Great One,
Inviting me to play around her jeweled breast
Open arms and breathe beauty and wonder
Music of the spheres is playing love songs
Nature warmly embraces grateful lovers
Listen as Moses and Jesus listened to eternity
Let their harmonious faith comfort and heal
Weeping endures for the night
Joy comes in the morning!

The rainbow gives the mountains an Easter greeting

Rainbow

I wake with rainbow skiing down
snow capped mountains

Quivering leaves catch the glow
trembling in awe

I walk in the light
glad to see the beauty of another day

Birds offer songs of praise
I join the chorus

God said, let there be light!

The angels in heaven showed me
rivers of fire from the throne of God.

The river flowed around
and above the trees

The whole sky blazed
with the light of God!

If you are walking through dark valleys
Jesus said, I am the light!

Lift your eyes to heaven's light.
Walk in the light of a new day!

True love knows no racial or cultural boundaries.
As sunlight falls on every mountain peak,
It freely falls on each and every person.

I turn off the Breaking News
of mob violence in city streets.

Walk toward the sunrise
gazing into the blazing fire of mystery.

Being cleansed, and
rising above society's imperfections.

The dawning of a new day—
Tenderness and healing is possible.

The warm light falls on my cheeks.
I fall on my knees filled with praise!

The ice blue mountains of Alaska
are so beautiful, so very beautiful!

There is no blue
like the ice blue mountains.

When God placed the blue moon
In the blue night time sky,

the mountain blue bird
was asked for advice!

The blue bird
broke into song.

Part II

The ice blue mountains of Alaska
are so beautiful, so very beautiful!

They are the vision
that gleamed in God's mind.

The vision shined in
the mountain blue bird's eye.

The mountains were called to rise,
rise high into the blue bird sky.

As a special touch,
the Poet of the world

placed the blue moon
In the blue night time sky.

The mountain blue bird
broke into song!

Part III

There is no blue
Like the mountain blue bird.

When God placed the blue moon
In the blue night time sky

The vision that gleamed in God's mind
Shined in the mountain blue bird's eye

The mountain blue bird
broke into song!

River of Hope

River of Fire flows—
Rushing across morning sky!
Come sacred altar.
Purify world of all sin.
Let faith, hope, and love blaze forth!

The light in Alaska is so beautiful,
so very beautiful!

As the sun rises licking the ice crystals,
turning them purple, mauve, and golden,
I begin to muse—

What is time?
Can you crawl into it?

Jacob's dream ladder
would be nice!

In these awe inspiring moments—
Time does stand still.

The world becomes so beautiful
our soul cracks open.

Letting the glory in!

  In nature there are

      Those moments

  When heaven and earth

      Become one

  One magnificent planet

      Wedded in wondrous

  Luminescent love

The dream that brought the first morning
shines with the brightness of a new day.
Live in beauty and goodness.
Fly with wings of faith, hope, and love.

Because once someone
dared to incarnate You
I will incarnate You too.

After another snowy day

and bone chilling night,

the sun triumphantly rose

as the song birds knew it would!

They rose from their snow tunnels.

Fluffed their down sleeping bags.

Lifted their wings in jubilation!

My soul took wing and flew.

Skies filled with lenticular clouds

ribbons of beauty and delight

Provide dreams for an eternity.

I'll lie here and contemplate

heaven's light pouring down

feel my soul ablaze.

Haibun Hope

If you are feeling discouraged,

sit quietly and meditate

on the magic of an Alpenglow sunrise.

Hear wings whisper inspirational Hope.

The person who breathes in Beauty

will never grow old.

Come and shine on me

Illumine with Heaven's Light

For I am fading

(A Haibun is a literary form originating in Japan that combines prose and haiku. My prose portion is only 6 lines, but the range of Haibun is broad and frequently includes autobiography, diary, essay, prose poem, short story, or travel journal. Haiku has a 5-7-5 format. The haiku poem consists of just three lines, with 17 syllables in total. The emphasis is on economy of words, and the syllable count can vary slightly. The first and third lines have 5 syllables. The second line has 7 syllables. Haiku is often the first form of teaching children poetry. Try it with your children or grandchildren. It is a lot of fun.)

Keep beauty in your heart
and you will never grow old.

Heard spruce tree praying
Standing proud as setting sun
Beams its approval

One after another
They fall from the snowy sky
Red cap flashing
Iridescence catching fire
The thrill of finding heart seeds

(Alpenglow can illumine red capped birds as well as snow capped mountains)

I usually label sunrise photos
as Alpenglow, but these two seem to
be closer to Aurora.
Aurora is a natural electrical phenomenon
characterized by streamers of reddish and purplish light in the sky.
The night time Aurora does usually have a lot of green.

Front Porch Art Show

Snow covered spruce
Lifting arms in joyous praise
Knees bowing in awe

(Sunset photos after 20 inches of new snow)

God's beautiful art show in progress
as we ski out of our garage
on to park trail by our condo

Time stands still
What is time?

Past lives in present
Inspired by future hope.

God's Home

*I am poverty. I am solitude.
I renounced spirituality to find God
Who preaches loudly
beside the running waters.
—Thomas Merton*

While the man-made
church houses are closed
Go into God's home
the world of nature
Dreamed and crafted by angel's hands
You will find God's birds and flowers
preaching joyful goodness and love
Butterflies and bees singing anthems of praise
In a sanctuary where kindness
is the stained glass windows
greater than the Sistine Chapel ceiling
painted by Michelangelo
Nature's Alpenglow clouds
gather the light of heaven's dome
Shine on all God's creatures
The doors to this chapel
are always open
The grassy sod is the plush carpet
Welcome mat inviting all to worship

View from my bedroom window after
hearing of the death of my 93 year old sister
in Georgia (not due to Covid-19). How could I not see it
as heaven shining brighter with her presence.

With the COVID-19 virus still raging,
we could not go to Georgia
to be with our dear family for graveside service.
I sent this poem as an expression of love for our family.

Robbie Dear

Robbie lived 93 years and 3 days.
As the oldest child in our large family,
Robbie took on the mothering role very early.

After mother's death in 1991, at age 83,
in addition to caring
for her children, Edwin and Edie,
and their growing families,
Robbie increased her caring
for the Cole clan.

From opening her home
for family gatherings,
to calling people on their birthdays. Today she is
Celebrating with our heavenly family.

We miss our family who
have gone on to heaven.
Yet they are with us every day
in loving ways.

For heaven is not far away,
not measured in years.
Heaven is in our joys,
and in our tears.

Heaven and earth
are not separate realities.
Heaven is family.
Family is forever.

> "I will be kind. . . . I will bless you
> with a future filled with hope."
> —Jeremiah 29:10-11 (CEV)
> "God's love and kindness
> will shine upon us
> like the sun that rises in the sky."
> —Luke 1:78 (CEV).

I am praying for all who are filled with fear and suffering.
May God's goodness and kindness sustain you,
replacing your fear with adventurous faith and hope
seen in each new golden sunrise!

I go into nature
for solace and find healing,
broken and find wholeness.

I go out pulled in many directions,
and return home peaceably centered
in God's goodness, grace, and love.

Thank you, God,
for the many gifts of nature.
Your window revealing heaven's glory.

If eyes are made for seeing

then beauty needs no other reason for being

Conclusion to Alpenglow Miracles: Fire Dance of Wonder

Sunrises and sunsets inspire me
to fill the space between them
with beauty, wonder, and kindness.

These Alpenglow miracles
have been written to energize and give shape
to our lives of faith and our world.

Our oneness with God and the world,
especially our oneness with all humankind,
ripens as we experience miracles
of beauty and wonder.

May we live our lives
in ever widening circles
that span our globe—
Become songs of redemption!

Embrace God,
not in robes of power, but
in relational transforming kindness.

Kindness is the language
known around the world.

Concluding Praise

Praise God for wonderful deeds
too marvelous to understand.

Praise God with dancing
and musical instruments.

Let every living creature
sing praises to God!

Other Books by Dwayne Cole

A Center that Holds: Adventures in Kindness
A Prayer of Blessing: As You Go Remember This
A Relational Hermeneutic of Kindness
A Relational Trinity of Kindness
BEARS AND MOOSE OF ALASKA: Nature Poetry
Down on the Farm in Georgia: A Poetic Memoir
Dragonfly Magic
Gentle Galilean Glories: The Tender Teachings of Jesus
God and Evil: An Ode to Kindness
Jesus Transforming Beatitudes: Selected Sermons from Year A
Jesus Transforming Love: Selected Sermons from Year B
Jesus Transforming Gentle Teachings: Selected Sermons from Year C
Kindness Is Every Step.
Poems Inspired by Process Philosophy
Poet of the Universe: A Vision of Beauty and Goodness.
The Apostles Creed: A Living Creed for the Living Church
The Book of Revelation: Jesus Kindness Transforms Suffering
The Serenity Prayer: A Pathway to Peace and Happiness
The Story of the Bible: Authority, Inspiration, Canonization, and Translation
TREES AND DRIFTWOOD: Poetic Ecology
WINGS OF INSPIRATION

www.ingramcontent.com/pod-product-compliance
Lightning Source LLC
Chambersburg PA
CBHW041215070526
44579CB00001B/3